IMPACT

The Story of Dr. Robert Pace
and His Comprehensive Musicianship as Taught
and Loved in Colorado and Throughout the World

Lois Tschetter Hjelmstad

Other Books by Lois Tschetter Hjelmstad

*Fine Black Lines: Reflections on Facing Cancer,
Fear and Loneliness*

*The Last Violet: Mourning My Mother,
Moving Beyond Regret*

This Path We Share: Reflecting on 60 Years of Marriage

Abidance: A Memoir of Love and Inevitability

All of Lois' books are available online, from bookstores, and at *www.loishjelmstad.com*

IMPACT

Lois Tschetter Hjelmstad

Mulberry Hill Press
Englewood, Colorado

Impact: The Story of Dr. Robert Pace and His Comprehensive Musicianship
as Taught and Loved in Colorado and Throughout the World
by Lois Tschetter Hjelmstad

Copyright ©2020 by Lois Tschetter Hjelmstad

All rights reserved. This book or parts thereof may not be reproduced in any form, stored in a retrieval system, or transmitted in any form by any means—electronic, mechanical, photocopy, recording, or otherwise—without prior written permission of the publisher except for the inclusion of brief quotation in a review.

Disclaimer: The information in this book is true and complete to the best of our knowledge. The author and/or publisher do not assume any responsibility for errors, omissions, or interpretation of the subject matter herein.

Published by
Mulberry Hill Press
2710 South Washington Street, Suite B
Englewood, Colorado 80113-1679
www.loishjelmstad.com
lois.hjelmstad@gmail.com

Editorial assistance: Barbara Munson
Cover and page design: Nick Zelinger
Cover photograph: James Lyke
The following was originally published as indicated:
"Close the Gate Gently" in *This Path We Share: Reflections on 60 Years of Marriage*, p. 192
Name: Hjelmstad, Lois Tschetter, author.
Title: Impact/Lois Tschetter Hjelmstad. —1st Ed.
p.cm.
Identifiers: ISBN 978-0-9637139-4-0
Library of Congress Control Number: 2020935962

Subjects: 1. Colorado Pacesetters. 2. Dr. Robert Pace.
3. Hjelmstad, Lois Tschetter. 4. Comprehensive Musicianship.
5. Pace Piano Method. 6. Robert Pace Piano Books. 7. Music for Piano.
8. Finger Builders. 9. Teaching Piano. 10. Pace Ensemble Festivals.
11. Pace Composition Festivals. 12. Pace Consultants.
13. Piano Studio. I. Title.

Printed in the United States of America
8 7 6 5 4 3 2 1

*To Pace consultants, teachers,
parents, and students everywhere—
with much love*

It's all about the process…

Creative development of ourselves and students
Process orientation
Balance between cognitive, affective, psychomotor
Music learning as a cognitive process
Implementation of dyads and group dynamics
Multi-key approach (tactile awareness)
Knowledge gained by teaching oneself and peers
Indirect transfer of learning
Spiral learning – deeper and broader immersion

– Core Values as Outlined by Dr. Robert Pace

Contents

A Book? *Really?* 11
An Enduring Legacy 14

The 1950s
    History of the 50s 21
    Flying with Dr. Pace – *Joan Reist* 22

The 1960s
    History of the 60s 27
    An Amazing Man 28
    A Structure for Thinking 33
    Something Different – *Delta Barker Bement* 34
    I COULD Do It 39
    I Am Only One 41
    The Best Laid Plans – *Marsha Wolfersberger* 42

The 1970s
    History of the 70s 49
    If It's Thursday Morning... 53
    Why We Teach Comprehensive Musicianship ... 55
    A Family Endeavor 56
    If Only – *Susan Rudosky* 58
    A Thinking Boy's/Girl's Approach 62
    Serendipity – *Darlene Harmon* 63
    Recitals – Every Day, All Week 65

The 1980s

- History of the 80s 69
- Quite Spry 71
- No Way – *Arlyce Black* 73
- What's Not to Love? 76
- Quotes and Tips from Dr. Pace 77
- Please, Please, No 79
- Like Mother, Like Daughter – *Kathy Van Arsdale* ... 82
- He Made Us Smile 86

The 1990s

- History of the 90s 89
- Second Generation – *Cindy Allor* 90
- A Trip to Rockley's Music Center 92
- Dr. Pace on Creativity 94
- Bad Dream, Good Ensembles 95
- How and Why We Stayed Together 97
- Five Girls and a Baby 99

The 2000s

- History of the 2000s 103
- Lexi and Dr. Pace – *Bonnie Early* 105
- Some Reasons Why We Began to Fade 106

The 2010s

- History of the 2010s 111
- We Lost Our Mentor 113
- But Even as We Faded... 114
- I Teach, Therefore I Am – *Kathleen Davis* 117

Group Reunion 118
　　Close the Gate Gently 119

APPENDICES
　　1. Consultants 121
　　2. What to Do After the Doctor Comes 123
　　3. Dr. Pace's Visits to the West 131
　　4. Sampling of Pace Festivals 133

ACKNOWLEDGMENTS 137
ABOUT THE AUTHOR 139

A Book? *Really?*

On a frosty morning in November 2018, my husband, Les, and I drove to Consultant Kathy Van Arsdale's lovely home for a Colorado Pace Legacy meeting.

We enjoyed banana bread and tea while the group of nine or ten current and former Colorado Pacesetters (as we teachers of the Robert Pace Comprehensive Musicianship Method had named ourselves) discussed ways in which we could preserve, send forward, and pay tribute to Dr. Pace's good work as well as celebrate our own commitment.

The group had been meeting for some months: each one turning in their own original handouts to send to Dr. Cindy Pace (his daughter), for her archives; as well as rounding up quotes from Dr. Pace's seminars and classes, finding Festival programs, and wondering what to do with more than fifty years of Pacesetter minutes.

I wasn't quite sure why Les and I had been invited. I had retired from teaching piano a good fifteen years earlier, after I wrote my first book and began speaking about breast cancer throughout the United States.

But there we were. It was good to see my old friends. Talking about Dr. Pace and his advanced pedagogical ideas reminded me how much I had loved teaching Comprehensive Musicianship over the years. For a moment I wished I were still teaching, although at age eighty-eight, as primary caregiver for my ninety-seven-year-old husband, as well as with my own health issues, the wish was only for the *briefest* of moments.

During the meeting, we tossed around the idea of perhaps putting our over-fifty-year-history-as-Pacesetters into some sort of a book. Everyone became excited. *Of course, a book!* Then, those seated around the dining room table stopped talking.

I looked at Les; he looked at me. A book. I had written four books. Could I write another, given my responsibilities, my struggles with chronic fatigue syndrome, my aches and pains? Les nodded ever so slightly. *Go ahead, my love, I'll support you.*

"*I* write," I announced. "I can do it."

As we left the meeting that day, I carried three huge notebooks of meeting minutes out to the car, then I went back to help Les down the flagstone walk. When we got home, I stashed the notebooks in the closet of my office. I needed first to concentrate on our family Christmas. Which came and went.

Another meeting had been scheduled for January 10, so I spent two entire weekends and several weekdays going through the minutes, taking notes, and pondering. I presented a few ideas to the group and asked for suggestions and more input.

By the March meeting I had written several little stories illustrating Dr. Pace's concepts, worked with his quotes that the members had submitted, and constructed several tables as Appendices. I asked for additional material.

Toward the end of March, I contracted a terrible human pneumo-virus. After I'd spent more than ten days in bed, Les became ill also and, in two days, we were both in Porter Adventist Hospital in Denver. A week later we were both transferred to Life Care Center of Littleton for three weeks of rehab. Then we came home to a month of Home Health Care in May.

In addition, a year earlier I had been diagnosed with macular degeneration and it was now obvious that my vision was deteriorating at a faster pace. (No pun intended.)

I resumed my compiling and writing in July. The work was a good way to spend the hot summer months. I decided that, although others have shared their thoughts and experiences, I would write in my voice. This book is my personal interpretation of the notes and my own recollections. In some cases, I have made small edits to the letters sent to me.

In order to provide some background for the long story of our Pacesetter group and the letters from consultants, I offer this short biography of Dr. Pace, written by his daughter, Dr. Cindy Pace, printed in the October 2011 issue of *Clavier* magazine:

An Enduring Legacy
by Dr. Cindy Pace

Dr. Robert Pace is credited with having, in many ways, revolutionized the art of piano teaching in the twentieth and twenty-first centuries, with his landmark ideas on both content and presentation.

As an educator, he passionately committed himself to helping students become independent learners and lifelong musicians. His vision of teaching music through simple ideas that could be infinitely interrelated, reshaped, and revisited has left an enduring legacy.

Early Years

Robert Pace was born on June 22, 1924, in Newton, Kansas, the county seat of Harvey County, Kansas, about twenty-five miles north of Wichita. During his childhood, he lived with his family on a farm, and later, in town. His mother was a former schoolteacher. His father owned a hardware store and, subsequently, a meat processing plant, and then a gift shop, which both of his parents operated.

Robert began piano lessons at the age of five, and by the time he was nine, was performing radio concerts three times a week, along with his violinist sister, Mary.

In addition to playing the piano, he also played trombone in his Junior High and High School Bands. He was a great fan of Glenn Miller and sought to emulate the master's sound in his trombone playing.

During these years, Robert also played baseball, breaking a finger as a result, and worked at several jobs, including delivering newspapers and selling poultry and eggs.

During his high school years, Robert became serious about his piano studies, and competed in and won many competitions. In 1942, he graduated from Hutchinson High School and was accepted as a scholarship student by Josef and Rosina Lhevinne for study with them at Juilliard School of Music.

The Army, Juilliard, and Beyond

Robert's Juilliard studies were almost immediately interrupted, for three years, when he was drafted into the army in 1943. As a Corporal, he served in the infantry in Germany, France, and Austria until 1945. After that, he became a lifelong pacifist.

Upon resuming his Juilliard studies with Rosina Lhevinne, one of the most noted pianists of the twentieth century, in early 1946 (her husband Josef died in Dec. 1945), Robert met and soon married Juilliard scholarship vocalist Helen Crabtree. Robert and Helen are thought to be the first couple of married Juilliard students to have graduated from that institution.

Helen collaborated with Robert on books and recordings throughout their life together until she became disabled by illness in 1998. The marriage between Robert and Helen lasted 62 years, until her death in 2009. They had four children, six grandchildren, and three great grandchildren.

Career

After Robert earned a Bachelor of Science degree at Juilliard, he received a master's and doctoral degree from Teachers College, Columbia University. He taught at Juilliard and subsequently at Teachers College where he became head of piano instruction in 1952, then Chairman of the Music Department in 1969. Along with teaching at Teachers College and developing materials for piano teaching, Dr. Pace was national piano chair of the Music Educators National Conference from 1953 to 1956.

During this time, he also concertized, appearing at the Isabella Stewart Gardner Museum in Boston, with the Dow Symphony Orchestra in Midland, Michigan, and in other performances throughout the country.

From 1959 to 1962, he was piano editor for the *Music Journal*. In 1962, he was appointed by President John F. Kennedy to the original four-member panel charged with studying music and music education in the United States. He served in this capacity until 1963, when the committee was discontinued after the assassination of President John F. Kennedy.

In 1963, Dr. Pace became director of the National Piano Foundation upon its inception. He served there fifteen years, until 1977, when he became executive director of the International Piano Teaching Foundation.

His Legacy

Dr. Pace received the 2003 Music Teachers National Association Achievement Award; an honorary Doctor of Music degree from Westminster Choir College, Princeton, New Jersey; and, in 2008, the Lifetime Achievement Award from the Music Educators National Conference. His books and articles have been translated into many languages and are distributed throughout the world.

Dr. Pace is renowned for his work developing "peer-teaching" piano lessons; for his curriculum of "Comprehensive Musicianship" in which he organically integrated repertoire, technique, reading and transposing, composing and improvising, analysis, theory, and musicality; for the development of his Multi-Key approach; for his philosophy of life-long independent musical learning; and for his abiding concern with the relationship between musical experience and its contribution to the quality of life of the individual and, in turn, society as a whole.

(Written by Dr. Cindy Pace, reprinted from the October 2011 issue of *Clavier* with permission.)

History of the 50s

In the 1950s, prominent names included our president, Dwight D. Eisenhower, Joseph Stalin, Winston Churchill, Charles de Gaulle, and General Douglas MacArthur.

The Korean War raged from 1950 – 1953. The United States lost 33,742 American soldiers, 92,134 were wounded, and 80,000 were missing in action (MIA) or prisoner of war (POW).

Teenagers dressed rebelliously in overtly sexual ways with tight trousers and leather jackets. Pope Pius XII declared the Assumption of Mary as dogma. The first transistor computer was built at the University of Manchester in 1953.

Some people see the 50s as the Golden Age of television. I wouldn't know. Our family did not have a TV until 1963. Les and I wanted all our children to be able to read before we got one.

And I really did not notice much of that history, as I spent the 1950s bearing and raising four children. I stayed home in those post-WWII years, like the 50s society expected, nay dictated, that women do. "Get Rosie the Riveter back in her home where she belongs."

However, Pace Consultant Joan Reist broke that mold, bigtime. She was busily getting educated.

And she first met Dr. Pace in the 50s, well predating the Colorado beginnings of the Pace movement, so I share her lovely letter here even though her involvement with Dr. Pace goes far beyond the 50s:

Flying with Dr. Pace – *by Joan Reist*

I first heard of Robert Pace when I was a freshman in college at the University of Nebraska-Lincoln in 1953. John Blythe, who was finishing his doctorate at Columbia Teachers College, was my piano teacher. He had a group of young students for us to observe, and sometimes teach, as he expounded on the Pace philosophy.

When I began teaching piano, I inherited one of Dr. Blythe's class members. He was one of the best students I ever had. He spent his professional life as oboe/English horn specialist with the Omaha Symphony and Mannheim Steamroller and as a public-school teacher in Omaha. If he hadn't had a "gig" on the day of my 80th birthday celebration, I would have invited him and he would have played his favorite piece—a Bartok Bear Dance!

My first personal encounter with Dr. Pace was at a workshop at the University of Kansas in the early 60s. I participated in his demonstration. That convinced me to utilize his group piano and partner lesson concept with his Comprehensive Musicianship philosophy in my newly developing studio, which successfully survived for more than thirty years.

When Dr. Pace presented a workshop in Lincoln, Nebraska, there was a clamor for a pedagogy class. He looked at me and said, "You can do it!" After I recovered from the shock, I put together a class and that began Pacesetters in Lincoln and Omaha.

Over the years I have had the opportunity to conduct many Pace pedagogy classes and lead creative festivals. I credit Dr. Pace with encouraging and instructing me in that aspect of my teaching career. I received a scholarship to attend Teachers College for a summer session.

One of the most important results of Dr. Pace's ingenuity—and creativity—was the development of the National Piano Foundation, which later became the International Piano Teaching Foundation (IPTF).

In keeping with the concept of peer learning and teaching, the individuals who became consultants learned from and taught each other. Much of my expertise has come from these contacts; many became dear friends.

I flew with Dr. Pace in his own plane, drove him to sessions—and almost drowned him in the Missouri River while trying to find his hotel in Sioux City, Iowa. We became good friends, and he never missed an opportunity to teach me. Once at a stop light that I wasn't paying attention to, he said, "Joanie, it will never get any greener!"

Dr. Pace's philosophy and forward thinking annoyed some traditional educators, members of MTNA in particular. However, he eventually overcame that disdain. When I was in MTNA leadership, I nominated him for its highest award, which he received.

And now, my best wishes to the Colorado Pace Teachers and my gratitude for your pursuit of an historic document to honor one of music's most outstanding educators. – **Joan Reist**

Wow.

As I read Joan's piece and those of the other Pace consultants included in this book, their accomplishments and contributions amaze me. I feel humbled to have been their colleague.

Dr. Pace has had a tremendous impact on each of us and the letters show that those writers have carried that influence throughout our country and out into the world.

And those of us also in the trenches, teaching each week—early in the morning, after school, often until eight or nine at night—have impacted our students in ways we may never know.

In this book, I will share some vignettes from my own life and studio. Perchance I can show a small slice of how Dr. Pace's extraordinary ideas worked in an everyday studio, how we teachers of Colorado Pacesetters benefited from his persona and utilized his teachings. He was an inspiration to everyone—and anyone.

Now, on to the histories, the letters, the quotes and tips. And as I weave in bits of my story, I hope they bring back memories of your own studios, your own participation, and your own love of the legacy of Dr. Robert Pace.

History of the 60s

Joan Reist was lucky there in Nebraska.

Colorado was not introduced to Dr. Pace until he gave a Saturday session workshop at the University of Denver in October 1963. DU professors followed up on that seminar with continuing instruction.

Coloradan Barbara Rembe founded Colorado Pacesetters in l964 or 65. Kathleen Davis joined the group in 1966. Ruth O'Neal and I joined in 1968.

Dr. Pace was in Colorado for a two-week seminar in Aspen in 1968, another one week in 1969, and two more weeks in Snowmass in 1970.

In the real world, the 1960s were turbulent: John F. Kennedy's election and death; the Cuban Missile Crisis; student protests; the assassinations of Robert Kennedy and Martin Luther King, Jr.

But the Pace movement was just getting started in Colorado. Let the world go by. We were looking at new adventures....

An Amazing Man

"This man is amazing," I thought, as I peered up at the stage from the cool darkness of an auditorium at the University of Denver. It was a scorching afternoon in the late summer of 1963 and Dr. Pace was sharing startling new concepts. Who would have thought to teach all twelve five-finger positions on the piano from the beginning?

Everyone I knew, myself included, first taught pieces in the key of C, no sharps or flats, then G (one sharp), then the key of D (two sharps), and then, at a much later date, A, E, B, and, maybe, after a few years, F# and C#. Same thing with flats; we always started with the key of F. But Dr. Pace was saying to teach all twelve five-finger positions right away.

He also told our audience to teach key signatures by starting with six sharps and six flats and dropping one at a time. That way the students see the whole picture and the patterns. I was astounded at the simplicity, the clarity, and the beauty of it.

Everything Dr. Pace said that afternoon resonated with me: Here was a way to teach that included everything that had concerned me since I had rather accidentally begun teaching two years earlier.

My daughter, Karen, and I were already taking piano lessons when my oldest son, Bobby, age seven, wanted to learn. There was no recourse but to teach him myself since we could not afford additional lessons. Soon neighborhood kids and relatives started coming to our house for piano lessons. And before I knew it, I had a dozen or so students.

I instinctively knew that there had to be more to teaching than opening a spiral notebook and looking at what we had covered the week before, as my teachers did. I knew there must be theory that I needed to include, but I didn't know what it was and there wouldn't have been enough time during lessons if I had. My earliest teachers had simply skipped over the pages that had scales or chords on them.

Every word Dr. Pace spoke rang an "Oh, yes" in my mind and heart. His theories of education and living were nothing short of brilliant.

Totally inspired, I drove home, excited to learn more when the DU professors provided follow-up in September.

But I needed surgery in early September. Then Les came down with mumps. During the next five weeks all three boys and I did, too. The semester was ruined. I did not get to learn more.

So, I began attending the Englewood Music Club meetings that fall, which were interesting and informative, but I was not learning what I needed to know—how to provide theory for my students, a structure upon which to hang the lessons.

A few years later, in June 1967, I went to a Pace workshop, again at DU, which further inspired me. Then, in early 1968 I jumped at a chance to participate in a Comprehensive Musicianship class, taught by Bonnie J. Cannalte, who was a consultant for this same Dr. Robert Pace. The eight-week session, thoroughly covering Books I and II, became an opportunity to outline each book. I outlined. Then I set the books in the bottom drawer of my desk. Maybe later.

That's the story of my first introduction to the work of Dr. Pace. This was Kathleen Davis':

The first time I encountered Dr. Pace was as a senior piano major at Oberlin Conservatory. Dr. Pace presented a workshop for a large contingent of piano pedagogy students. At the time I was impressed, probably taken aback, by his energy. I remember him charging up and down the aisles of the lecture hall flashing music note cards at us, appalled at how slow the music majors were to name the lines and spaces!

Susan Rudosky also shared hers:

I was teaching at Lewis and Clark College's Preparatory Music School in Oregon when I attended my first workshop with Dr. Pace. Everything he said hit home for me: conceptual learning; transposing and improvising right from the beginning; the support within small groups and partner lessons; understanding how melodies are built, and why the chords work as they do; how music is put together.

I signed up immediately for the Music for Piano Level I course, spread over six weekends, taught by IPTF consultant Connie Dean. I loved it, and that following summer of 1977, I attended a wonderfully inspiring teachers' workshop with Dr. Pace in Santa Fe, New Mexico.

Bonnie Early told this story of how she met Robert Pace:

> Dr. Pace gave a three-day workshop at San Jose University in 1976 (I believe). I decided to go and I was so enthralled that I could hardly contain myself.
>
> First of all, I thought that I would literally give ANYTHING to learn to teach like that. Secondly, I thought it sounded overwhelming; I wasn't sure I could ever do it. I moved to Colorado in 1977 and when I found out there were Pace teachers and consultants here, I hooked up with them and started taking classes. I was pregnant and had a baby during the first class (well, not in the class per se). I was in the hospital for a while and very sick and weak. I found out much later that they hadn't expected either me or the baby to live.
>
> I went through a divorce shortly after that, right about the time I was taking the second class. Needless to say, I missed part of the lessons and didn't get much out of them. Eventually I took all the classes from Level I through Level V/VI twice, many from Ruth O'Neal and a few from Kathleen Davis and Kathy Van Arsdale. Now teaching comprehensively is as easy as breathing, but it took a long time to get there.

And from Kathy Van Arsdale:

> I had been teaching Pace for a year and finishing Level I certification. I was determined to meet this genius! That opportunity came at a social event at my parents' house.

Dr. Pace had come to Denver to facilitate a Musicianship Festival. Although he began his career by playing on local radio in Kansas, Robert Pace was now an elegant, erudite New Yorker.

At that gathering, Dr. Pace was open to discussing any question put to him and was genuinely interested in each questioner. He came across as relaxed, humorous, and engaging. I couldn't wait for his session with local teachers the next day.

Lucky, lucky Kathy! Lucky, lucky us!

A Structure for Thinking by Dr. Pace:

Compare

Summarize

Observe

Classify

Interpret

Critique

Imagine

Hypothesize

Apply

Make choices

The brain can't send a message unless there is a structure.

Something Different

Everything I know about Consultant Delta Barker Bement is good. We were condo-mates one of the summers I spent at Dr. Pace's seminars in Snowmass, Colorado. She was well-organized, willing to help, and incredibly enthusiastic. I took several Book Five and Book Six courses from her; she was an excellent teacher. And, as seen in her letter, her impact has reached several continents:

In the summer of 1966, just after my husband and I had moved from California to Colorado, a friend asked me to give piano lessons to her five children. I was hesitant, telling her that it had been some time since I had taught and that I was not up on the latest in pedagogy techniques and literature. She insisted.

So, in the summer of 1968 I began attending piano seminars all over the Denver, Boulder, Fort Collins, and Greeley areas to see what was new. I found that most of the presenters were selling music.

Then I attended a seminar at Regis College in Denver featuring Dr. Robert Pace from Columbia University in New York. **Now here was someone and something different. Something that was new, exciting, based on educating the child, not selling music.** *I was hooked and opened a studio that eventually grew to eighty students, with assistance from four certified Pace teachers.*

Although I had three young children, all of whom were in my studio and musically active in their schools, I devoted myself to the concepts taught by Dr. Pace. I spent many hours preparing two lesson plans for each weekly class—a fifty-minute class plan and a forty-minute partner lesson plan.

Eventually Dr. Pace asked me to be a consultant; I taught Musicianship Pedagogy Courses locally as well as in other states. Seeing people grasp the goodness, logic, and appeal of this method excited me. We formed Study Groups after each course, which is one of the strengths of this method: teachers working and sharing together.

Dr. Pace was a dynamic charismatic person and teachers were drawn to him, but in addition, these bright teachers were drawn to the concepts he taught. He was on the cutting edge of new research about how people learn, and he shared this with us. It was most gratifying to watch young students of this method learn not only to play beautifully but also to understand what they were playing, to analyze the music, to improvise on it, and to compose pieces themselves. How much better can it get?

I arranged for Dr. Pace to give a workshop in Fort Collins at Colorado State University. He had developed materials to teach his method in the public schools. As a result, we began the program in four schools in Boulder, three public and one private. He came to observe, always anxious and curious to see how the program was working.

Dr. Pace's books were translated into Spanish and he shared these with me. I began the program in La Paz, Bolivia (with over 400 students in that city), as well as classes in Oruro and Tarija, Bolivia. Following this, I started the program in California with classes in the cities of Arcadia, Duarte, North Hollywood,

Burbank, and Los Angeles—comprising eighteen Spanish Groups and one Samoan Group. My last stop was in the Dominican Republic with classes in the cities of Santo Domingo, Barahona, and San Juan, where one of the students said, "Man, why can't we use parallel fourths? It sounds so neat."

These experiences reinforced my notion that people everywhere want to learn, not just to play a piece by rote, but to understand the music itself. Knowledge gave them power. In each location I spotted outstanding students and gave them a Musicianship Pedagogy Course so they could teach teachers. I did not want to come in, make a splash, and then leave, but rather to build a foundation so I would not even be missed when I left. As a result, Dr. Pace has a legacy in these places.

Dr. Pace emphasized conceptual learning—that we could apply concepts everywhere, see possibilities everywhere. I used this idea with a Children's Choir in Boulder where ten minutes of every rehearsal were spent learning music fundamentals. Children lined up at the piano and at the blackboard; choir mothers flashed cards to lines of other children.

The popular Dr. Jordan Peterson, Professor of Psychology at the University of Toronto, is currently writing and speaking about the concepts of order and chaos. People are listening.

*Well. Dr. Pace had already taught **us** about order—the sequential order of learning—particularly regarding chords. That is, begin not with 7th chords, but rather with the basis of a 7th chord, which is a triad. Then, when we understand major, minor, diminished, and augmented triads, then only, move on to 7th chords.*

He also showed us order in the compositions of Handel and Mozart. Their music contrasts sharply with some modern music which I find chaotic. As a result of learning about musical order and chaos, we can better see order and chaos in the world around us. Priceless.

There seemed to be no end to using Dr. Pace's model of creating concept sheets. For example, I made a concept sheet for every chapter in the Old and New Testaments, pulling out the concepts in each chapter and making a teaching sequence for those concepts. It was great fun although it took me ten years. Hundreds more ancient records are surfacing in many countries, including a library discovered at Nag Hammadi in Egypt, and the Dead Sea Scrolls in the Middle East.

In what other ways can we apply his model?

The Egyptians believed that we could keep chaos at bay with our minds. I have two former piano students who are incarcerated. The one in prison, in Sterling, Colorado, has access to a piano, but the one in jail, Mark, does not. Mark is practicing with his mind as Dr. Pace taught. What is that worth, for goodness sake?

Among his many gifts as a teacher of teachers, Dr. Pace had the capacity to accept teachers at whatever level they had attained, all the while offering a vision and encouraging individual growth.

For example, when I was teaching at Frankfurt High School in Germany, I had a serious skiing accident and lost the use of my left hand and arm. I recovered somewhat, but was never again a performer; however, I could still teach.

Dr. Pace accepted this, for which I am grateful. He was never arrogant, and I never saw him embarrass a student or teacher, which are important attributes for a teacher to have. He had the gift of optimism and faith in individual growth. Somehow, he made us want to grow, to expand our horizons.

Some teachers objected to his method. It was WORK!! Each week we made those fifty-minute class lesson plans and forty-minute partner lesson plans. Teaching in groups takes energy, especially if you have a junior high class. (One will be guaranteed a spot in Heaven if you teach that age group.) And it is certainly easier to teach one student at a time.

But the rewards are worth it: greater teacher knowledge, faster student learning, greater student and teacher satisfaction. We have learned an enormous amount from this great man. He was twenty-five years ahead of everyone else. I wish he had written his own book, explaining his concepts himself, so his message could have gone forth in his own words to many more people.

There is no limit to the ways and areas in which we can think conceptually, and we can continue to stretch our minds for a lifetime of learning. I desire greatly to pass this on. Dr. Pace lives on in our lives in a marvelous way.

– **Delta Baker Bement**

I *COULD* Do It

Meanwhile, back at the ranch. I (Lois) had set the Pace books aside. But then, and then....

Dr. Pace was coming to Colorado in July 1968 to give a two-week Pedagogy Course in Aspen. But, of course, I couldn't go. I had a seventeen-year-old daughter and sons aged fifteen, twelve, and ten at home. No way could I leave that wild crew for two weeks.

But as I ironed twenty-eight shirts one afternoon, I suddenly set down the iron and said out loud, "I COULD go."

That evening I mentioned the possibility to Les. He smiled and said, "If you really want to go, I'll manage everything here."

It was one of the most enlightening experiences of my life. The clean air in Aspen invigorated me. I loved eating out with my roommates, Irene Jurgenson and Carol Watson. And the classes…. The classes inspired, enthused, and left me determined. Dr. Pace was astonishing.

As luck would have it, one of the renowned Englewood teachers decided to retire that fall and referred some of her students to me. My studio suddenly enlarged from eighteen students to forty-five. And I transferred every one of them into Book One of Dr. Pace's method.

No matter what the students knew or at what level they played, Dr. Pace insisted that they start at the beginning of his series in order to lay the foundation of Comprehensive Musicianship. The older students continued playing at their stage of expertise, but they needed to learn to improvise, create variations, and understand the basics.

(One of my nieces went into Book One with the teen group. That class completed Book Two by spring. She went to college that fall and tested out of the first and second year of Theory. Eventually she earned her Master's Degree in Organ Performance and served a church as organist for many years.)

I assembled the students into age- and level- related Large Groups. I found partners for everyone. I discovered how difficult it was to make a schedule that worked for forty-five students and their parents. I popped a fair number of Excedrin.

But I did it.

One evening, about three months after the Aspen Conference, I bounded up the basement stairs, breathless, face aglow.

"I am so excited! The beginners got it—they understood the concept of up and down, high and low. Hey, you guys ready for dinner?" My three sons sniffed.

"We're starving. Why do you have to teach, anyway?" Son #3 was not a happy camper, even though I had been teaching him, plus #1 and #2 ever since they each turned seven.

"Well, it's partly because I want to help Dad. How do think we'd afford your violin lessons and orthodontia? And it's partly because I can."

"Yeah, but you like it," Son #2's tone was a bit accusatory.

"Yes, I like it. I love it. I know you'd like more privacy here in the house, but this is just the way it is." I smiled, stirred the chili, and spooned it into large green Melmac bowls.

They are in their 60s now, but they still play music. Turns out that they loved it, too.

I Am Only One

I am only one,
But still I am one.
I cannot do everything,
But still I can do something;
And because I cannot do everything,
I will not refuse to do
The something that I can do.
– Edward Everett Hale

Citation: Edward Everett Hale Quotes. BrainyQuote.com, BrainyMedia Inc, 2019.

https://www.brainyquote.com/quotes/edward_everett_hale_393297, accessed November 5, 2019.

The Best Laid Plans

Marsha Wolfersberger thanked the Pace Legacy Committee for the opportunity to take a trip down memory lane with us and other long-time devotees of Dr. Robert Pace. She wrote:

When my husband, John, and I left college and seminary in 1961 and took our first assignment in Overland Park, Kansas, I intended to be a mother and housewife/preacher's wife while my husband pastored a large church.

But I missed having a piano so much. When the salesman at Jenkins Music Store said I could pay for one by teaching piano students, I decided to try. My BA in Religious Education had not prepared me to teach piano, but I had played since second grade, so I figured, "How hard could it be!" It was painful. As soon as I paid off the piano, I quit.

Shortly thereafter, a college friend invited me to attend a workshop with Dr. Pace at University of Missouri at Kansas City. **He literally changed my life.**

I saw children with musical understanding and skills I had never imagined. I saw a dynamism in Dr. Pace that respected the students and gave them musical literacy and independence that was unlike any teaching I had ever experienced. I saw an approach to teaching that brought fresh new ideas for sight-reading, improvisation, harmonization, ear training, transposition, and technic that were both fun and effective.

I was hooked. I signed up then and there to take Contemporary Group Piano Teaching Sessions with Pat Lewis. Then I got cold feet and tried to back out, but there was no refund allowed—so I showed up.

John and I remodeled our garage into a studio with three pianos, where I taught several hundred piano students over the next fifteen years.

After taking many pedagogy classes, I started attending summer sessions at Columbia University with Dr. Pace in New York City. He appointed me as a Clinician for the National Piano Foundation in 1965. I did not feel qualified, but he said, "You can ultimately teach many more students by training teachers, than you can by just teaching students yourself." I accepted the challenge. The encouragement of Dr. Pace, colleagues like you, and many others I met through the National Piano Foundation [later called International Piano Teachers Foundation or IPTF] gave me the confidence to succeed.

I taught Pedagogy sessions for teachers in the Kansas City area; we had a strong group of Contemporary Piano Teachers. Dr. Pace came to conduct a Piano Ensemble Festival in 1974 that involved thirty-two teachers and five-hundred students. That experience was unique and memorable.

In the early 70s, Dr. Pace suggested we try a new Pedagogy Class for Public School Teachers. Through the public schools' Teacher Enrichment programs, we found an inroad to these teachers. We intended to show them how to teach music fundamentals in the classroom beyond the traditional "singing" approach. This was both a challenging and successful program.

It ultimately had over 50,000 public school students in the KC Area learning music fundamentals and having fun at the piano. Many of those classroom teachers then became private studio teachers as well, using the group teaching methods they had learned.

Besides all the pedagogy teaching, I was commuting to the University of Kansas, studying for my Master's in music education, and teaching class piano at KU.

In 1985, after years of taking three-week summer sessions in High Woods and New York City, I moved to NYC and served as Dr. Pace's assistant while completing my Doctoral studies. I graduated from Teachers College, Columbia University, with a Doctor of Education diploma with a specialty in Piano Pedagogy.

In the late 70s John and I moved to Indiana, where I taught Class Piano and Piano Pedagogy at Jordan College of Fine Arts at Butler University in Indianapolis until we moved to California in 1987.

This move enabled me to follow "greats" like John Blythe and Mitzi Kolar. I taught Piano Pedagogy and Class Piano at San Diego State University for five years. There I established a Community Music School as a place for budding piano teachers to be interns and learn to teach group piano.

Upon leaving San Diego, we moved to the Claremont, California area where I became faculty and then Executive Director of the Claremont Community School of Music for ten years until I retired in 2002. In this role, I continued to train Pace teachers, some of whom are still teaching.

Since retirement, I have been a Country Line Dance instructor in senior communities for seventeen years. My group teaching *experience has made this a comfortable place for me and helps keep me in shape.*

Dr. Pace was right: teaching teachers exponentially expanded the number of people I could ultimately teach. I taught not just the concept of group teaching, but his philosophy about the importance of making music available to all people—not only those already gifted.

His gracious acceptance of people as they are, where they are, and the reality that people learn in many ways, requiring us to teach in different ways, has infused my life's work.

*I have tried to multiply the number of teachers **I** trained by the number of teachers and students **they** taught, to estimate the number of lives Dr. Pace reached just by teaching **me**. When you multiply that by all of **you**, **HE** had a tremendous impact on this world. I am eternally grateful.*

Our four children all studied piano with Pace teachers and are life-long music lovers and performers. When we get together annually, they play violin, banjo, guitar, string bass, and sing, as well as play piano.

They exhibit the philosophy of Dr. Pace that learning to play piano conceptually allows you to transfer that to other instruments and is meant to give you a lifetime of musical enjoyment. He believed making music would make you a better human being. I remain in touch with many students who have confirmed this long-term result.

– **Marsha Wolfersberger**

History of the 70s

Colorado Pacesetters were going great guns by the early 1970s. We had a General Meeting every month and Study Groups *on each of the other three Thursdays.*

But at one Executive Board meeting several years later, the participants—Bonnie Cannalte, Louise Farley, Carolyn Heitzman, Wilhelmina Howe, Joy Jelinek, Irene Jorgensen, Ruth O'Neal, and Joan Wade—had to wonder if, due to the gas shortage and ensuing expense, we needed to consider meeting in geographical multi-level Study Groups. We had been working with groups who were all on the same level of expertise. Perhaps there could even be some advantages to heterogeneous groupings.

At the fall general meeting that year, it was suggested that the Pace teachers set a minimum fee for lessons. This would eliminate the unintentional undercutting of each other's studios and place a higher value on the lessons. It was moved, seconded, and passed that we recommend a minimum fee of $60 per quarter for a partner lesson and a large group each week.

The roster for 1973-74 listed thirty-six participants in six different Study Groups plus nine public school teachers who had taken at least one Pace Pedagogy Course.

By 1974, there were eighty teachers who had taken Comprehensive Musicianship courses. Many of them had joined Pacesetters.

We worked on by-laws that year. The minutes show that, at one meeting, one of our members made a motion that the wording of the by-laws be bisexual. Certainly, why not? Or did she mean bilingual? Or kind of a he/she mix?

Dues were $5.00. It was mandated that all Pace teachers also belong to Colorado State Music Teachers Association (CSMTA).

Two new consultants had been appointed: Ruth O'Neal, in Denver, and Sheila Rowe, in northern Colorado.

By 1975, Kathleen Davis had become a consultant. Ruth O'Neal and Karen Clifton spent three weeks at Teachers' College in New York, studying with Dr. Pace, Bert Konowitz, and Mary Pollard.

The dues were raised to $8.00.

We had hosted several large Pace Creative Workshops in the early years:

- thirty minutes of questions and answers, improvisation, and other creative activities
- fifteen minutes playing ensembles
- ten minutes of fundamentals games

Then, for some years, we opted for smaller inter-studio workshops instead.

However, Ruth O'Neal felt that we should once again hold good, general Creative Workshops every other year, because **we had two unique things to offer: Our teacher-training programs and our workshops.**

So, in March of 1976 the Executive Board planned another city-wide Creative Festival, to be chaired by Carolyn Heitzman and Louise Farley.

In 1977, Dr. Pace became head of the International Piano Teaching Foundation. That was also the year that Bonnie Early moved to Colorado and joined us. The 1977-78 roster listed sixty Pace teachers in Colorado.

In 1979, one of my students was a winner for the CSMTA Senior High Division. I also presented Creativity as a Way of Teaching at CSMTA with a group of my kids.

One of Ruth O'Neal's students, Yvan Greenberg, wrote a composition for the Colorado Symphony Orchestra.

In 1979, we changed our General Meeting to once every other month with Study Groups on the alternating months. The North, South, and West groups had been meeting on several Thursdays each month. Apparently two to four meetings a month had become onerous for our busy selves.

Dues were raised to $15.00.

The July 1979 Pacesetter Newsletter featured an important article by Pacesetter's president Lucille Koenig summarizing the discussion with Dr. Pace during his seminar at Rockley's Music Store:

According to Dr. Pace, the purpose of Pacesetters is 1) for your own development and 2) for professional development. Set goals and start working on them. Concentrate on the process. Meet as often as you can. Commit to being there; you can't be a Pacesetter and stand on the side. A group will splinter as soon as members of the group do not find satisfaction. We are not elitist, but we believe in very high standards.

As president of Pacesetters this year, I realize the some of the problems of the group are 1) gasoline prices and the distances we must travel for our meetings, 2) the new and former existing members have different goals, and 3) the demanding schedule a Pace teacher keeps.

But the important benefits we receive from being a member of this group should inspire us to make the commitment to help in whatever way we can.

Meanwhile, in the 1970s, troopers shot and killed four student protestors at Kent State; M*A*S*H* premiered; abortion was legalized; the Watergate scandal caused Nixon's resignation and Gerald Ford to become president; Microsoft was founded; Jimmy Carter became president; Iran held our hostages. And in Jonestown, Guyana, one of my uncles and his family, along with hundreds of others, drank Kool-Aid at the behest of Jim Jones—and died.

If It's Thursday Morning…

By this time, I had taken the courses for all six Pace books, some more than once. I no longer felt unqualified, (although no teacher has ever thought that he/she knows enough or has done enough).

I had finished the early morning lessons, tidied up the kitchen, and opened the door for my South Study Group friends, most of whom arrived promptly at 9:30. Pat was running late that morning, so she arrived sans makeup, apologizing profusely. Although she looked quite different, I thought she looked fine. It was just Study Group after all.

We settled in on the benches of my four pianos and started with Finger Builders from Book IV, diminished seventh arpeggios. Those not seated on a bench commented on hand positions and directed our dynamics.

My studio had two six-foot-long blackboards with permanent staves; we moved to the boards to write chord inversions.

Triad flash cards, augmented, major, minor, and diminished, followed.

We spent a half hour analyzing pieces in Music for Piano and thinking of ways to improvise on their concepts.

We lined up at the two front pianos for Questions and Answers, discovering how fast one must think, sympathizing with our students. It humbled us to realize what we expected from eight-year-olds.

At the end of the two hours, we hugged, said goodbye, and returned to our studios, better prepared to teach, eager to try the new ideas that we had shared.

Why We Teach Comprehensive Musicianship

- We can develop the habit of making ourselves and our students the center of our own learning.

- We are working ourselves out of a job by creating independent life-long learners.

- We are structuring meaningful experiences in our lives and in the lives of our students.

- We are learning from the inside out.

- We can open avenues in each student for musical exploration as a means of developing personal sensitivity, creative thinking, the ability to respond to and deal with environment and peers, and an ability to solve problems effectively.

A Family Endeavor

My studio designated the third Thursday in September as Back-to-Piano night. On my Policy Statement, I "required" the parents to attend. Of course, you can't make people do anything but most of them did come. Was it for the platters of cookies and punch? Or did they really want to hear about the Robert Pace Method?

I worked for days on my talk. I pulled quotes from inspiring writers and statistics from brain development books. I tried to insert a bit of wry humor where I could. I cut and pasted (actually, with real scissors and real glue) into the notebook that held my Back-to-Piano talks. Sometimes I re-used passages from the preceding ones. Maybe it was a foreshadowing of my yet-to-come public speaking career.

I really loved Back-to-Piano Night. I was passionate about teaching Dr. Pace's innovative Comprehensive Musicianship and enjoyed touting its advantages and simplicity to anyone who would listen.

I told about how a study had shown that, while only 10% of kids in the United States (this was back in the 70s and 80s) get a musical background, that 10% win 90% of all scholarships and awards. I hoped to make the parents feel good about making those multiple trips back and forth each week to my studio.

The parents of each Large Group, of course, met one another at the six-week recitals. B to P Night was a chance for all of them to engage. It made for a "family" feeling.

Speaking of families, I had a number of families where I taught more than one of their children.

One father remarked that, yes, he knew the way to my house. He had been coming four or five times a week. Over a period of eighteen years. His three daughters all studied from the time they were in second grade until they graduated from high school. The older two were taking lessons when the youngest was born. She had even come to recitals in utero. When Sara was about three, she was appalled when told she couldn't take lessons yet.

She stomped her little foot and said, "But I want to play a tonatina, too!"

Her parents were very conscientious about practice; the girls progressed well. They are all still involved in music and Sara, the small sonatina girl, is a professional soprano soloist and music teacher.

Probably every teacher has had multiples from one family. Either the olders inspire the youngers or the parents have a strict family policy of "You WILL study piano."

If Only…

Susan Rudosky's path to teaching the Pace Method wound through several states, out to Hawaii, and back to us. When the Legacy Committee put out the call for memories, Susan sent this interesting piece regarding that journey:

> I've always loved music and piano. I can remember wanting to take lessons when I was three, like my eight-and ten-year-old siblings. But their piano teacher said, "Not until she can read." When I did begin instruction, my lessons were traditional private lessons: note-reading, repetitive practice for perfection, and theory classes that did not correlate to the repertoire being studied or go any further than the assigned worksheets.
>
> **Thankfully, much in music education has changed since then. I have often wished I had been taught with the Pace approach when I was little. If only.…**
>
> I received my Master of Music degree in Piano Pedagogy from the University of Colorado-Boulder in 1975. There I had had classes in the group piano approach with Dr. Guy Duckworth; I agreed with some of his textbooks' emphasis on multi-key, modal experimentation, and improvisation, but somehow the Group Dynamics classes didn't click with me.
>
> My primary professor, Howard Waltz, used traditional individualized instruction and when I began teaching, I used what I hoped to be the best of both paths.
>
> Two years later, in 1977, I moved to Portland, Oregon, to teach at Lewis and Clark College's Preparatory Music School, where I attended my first workshop with Dr. Pace. It was my

"Aha!" moment. The lights turned on. I felt like I'd found The Way.

This understanding is real learning, not the cursory learning in which I'd spent years, thinking it was the best preparation for performance. I found when performing a piece that has been conceptually learned, there is a security when walking on stage. "I know this music; I know what I am doing," as opposed to the panicked feeling of "What's my luck going to be today? Will my fingers remember what to do?"

I signed up immediately for the Music for Piano Level I course, taught by IPTF Consultant Connie Dean. That summer, I attended an inspiring teachers' workshop with Dr. Pace in Santa Fe, New Mexico.

More courses followed: Moppets, Kinderkeyboard, Level II, Level III. I took as many as I could. I became active in the Portland Pacesetters, a terrific group of teachers who willingly shared their teaching successes and strategies at our monthly meetings. We took turns teaching and being the students, always carrying out Dr. Pace's philosophy and approach.

That was such a wonderful time; there was no ego involved among the teachers. During the two years there, we organized Festivals for our students—a Musicianship Festival and an Ensemble Festival. I also attended an Ensemble Festival in Seattle, with Dr. Pace as guest conductor. I attended workshops in San Francisco and at Teachers College, New York, each time realizing that this was/is the best way to learn and teach.

Dr. Pace believed strongly in the importance of music education, and how this affects our culture and society.

A voracious reader, he provided us with recommended book lists—from the latest on child development and how we learn, to socio-economic theories. He developed a devoted following of teachers world-wide.

Through his establishment of the International Piano Teaching Foundation, he modeled and imparted his beliefs through teacher training workshops. He emphasized, "Everyone has a strength to contribute to the group. We learn best, retain, and relate best with peer interaction."

In 1979, when I moved to Honolulu, I began teaching the Pace program, first at a piano dealership, and later at a private K-12 school. There were a few other Pace teachers in Honolulu, moving in and out. Two of us formed the Pacific Pacesetters.

We enjoyed our short time together, but it was a struggle to get other teachers interested. The local community of piano teachers had a high focus on competitions. Teaching the Pace approach mandated an "about face," with required teacher training, comprehensive lesson planning, goals for each semester, meetings for sharing....

In 1999 several of us organized an Ensemble Festival, with Dr. Pace as guest conductor. He was on his way to Japan and stopped in Honolulu. It was a highlight, a thrill to experience his kind, yet firm ways, with high expectations for the children. The children derived so much during the rehearsals and the performance—ten pianos, working together, following a conductor, playing expressively. The parents were thrilled and wrote lovely thank you notes. Those children will always remember this experience with fondness.

The groups of children in my studio blossomed and thrived. We had fun and worked hard. Some stayed together in the same group from Kindergarten through 8th grade. They lived and learned music the way it should be—comprehensively, with enjoyment, and with an understanding they will carry throughout their lives. That is our goal as teachers.

And that is what Dr. Pace gave me.

– **Susan Rudosky**

A Thinking Boy's/Girl's Approach

Dr. Pace insisted that The Arts are a viable way of learning anything—and everything. They are not "enrichment," they are *fundamental* to education.

He underscored:

- For our nation's future, it is vital to improve how persons can think.

- "Why music?" The problems we meet in society are like the problems we find in music.

- It is important to teach process because products change too quickly.

- It is also important to teach, not just piano, but musicianship, logic, patterns. It is the thinking person's method. We develop the whole person.

Serendipity

It often astounds any of us to realize how one moment, one choice, one serendipity can alter our lives. Darlene Harmon's engaging note illustrates that point:

By chance, my daughter's first piano teacher taught Pace. Little did I know that that choice would shape the next forty years of my own piano teaching and that her teacher would become my mentor and friend! Through my daughter's lessons, I became very interested in this comprehensive approach to learning to play the piano. After taking some exhilarating and thorough pedagogy classes, I was encouraged to switch my own students over to the Pace method. I never looked back.

I discovered that I could offer so much more to my students. My teaching had direction and new energy. I became part of a group of progressive thinkers—the Colorado Pacesetters. We had monthly meetings and additional monthly Study Groups. We had a festival every year, rotating between ensemble, composition, and creative themes.

Dr. Pace was part of our festivals and did Master Classes with our group. He had a true vision for teaching, a true passion for his methodology. With all I learned from Dr. Pace and the Pacesetter group, I was able to offer my students partner lessons and group theory classes.

My students thrived in this peer-based environment. They completed their piano studies with a well-rounded music education in addition to learning to play the piano. Being part of this method of teaching kept me excited and growing for all the years of my teaching career.

I will be forever indebted to Dr. Pace and the Pace teachers. And to the serendipitous choice of my daughter's piano teacher.

– **Darlene Harmon**

Recitals – Every Day, All Week

I loved, loved Recital Week. We invited parents and friends to attend every Large Group, where each class demonstrated what we had learned in the unit just completed.

The students played two-, four-, eight-person piano ensembles. They proudly performed their newest original compositions and repertoire pieces. They raced to write key signatures and triads at the big blackboards.

I held these individual class recitals in October, December, February, and March, approximately every six weeks, at the end of each division. In May we had a Big Spring Recital with all six or seven groups combined.

On Monday morning of one particular week in October, I had made the punch, ready to be iced, and placed the assorted cookies on a large tray covered with plastic wrap.

The six-thirty a.m. student, Rachelle, came running into the studio, blond curls bouncing. Her partner followed soon after. They did their *Finger Builders* in unison, then listened for expressiveness and watched for good hand position as they took turns playing the *Music for Piano* piece of the week.

As we proceeded to practice their duet, I noticed Rachelle looked a little green. When she whimpered, "Mrs. Hjelmstad, I don't feel good," I ran to get a wastebasket, but I was too late.

Rachelle upchucked all over her piano, vomit splattering on her books and seeping between the keys. I calmed her down, led her into the bathroom, and cleaned up her little face.

But what about the piano? And the recital that evening?

I called my technician. He hurried over, took the piano apart, and cleaned it up, saying, "I'll be back to put it together for the lessons and recital this afternoon. It'll have to dry overnight, so I'll take it apart again after the recital each day and put it together early in the mornings." Okaaaaay.

The recitals went well. The parents were delighted. Rachelle never threw up at my house again.

History of the 80s

To put the Pacesetter's 1980s in context, it might be helpful to know that, in the Decade of Greed: Ronald Reagan was elected president twice; John Lennon was shot; Mount St. Helens erupted; the AIDS plague was identified; PCs were introduced; the Challenger exploded; the Berlin Wall fell.

And lots of minutes were written at Pacesetter meetings. I read all of them while researching this book. (Of course I did.)

I saw that Carolyn Heitzman had chaired the 1980 Creative Workshop; I remembered that she did the scheduling for many festivals. She was one of the most organized people I have ever met.

I also noted that our dues were raised to $10 that year from the $8 in the '70s and the original $5.

Bonnie Cannalte, our first consultant, and Rosa Silver, a fervent and valuable member, both passed away in the summer of 1980. They had been such dedicated teachers and encouragers in our Pacesetters group; we missed them greatly. It was almost like the passing of Camelot.

Dr. Pace chose to hibernate for a year in order to write, revise, and attend to his Department Head position at Columbia University.

In 1981 Karen Golden joined us from Atlanta. In 1982 Hazel Roberts and Kathy Van Arsdale became Pace teachers and joined our group. In 1982 Janet Arnold's daughter, Jennifer, won first in the Sonatina Competition sponsored by the Foothills Music Teachers Association.

Kathy Van Arsdale became a Pace Consultant in 1984. For some length of time, she, Kathleen Davis, and Ruth O'Neal taught Comprehensive Musicianship classes at the University of Colorado-Denver.

However, some of the fervor of the 1970s had waned a bit. We often discussed how we could get more participation, even though the roster included many names of teachers who had taken at least one Pedagogy Course.

Quite Spry

As I said earlier, my studio (and many others) had Group Recital Weeks every October, December, February, and March. But the *pièce de résistance* for me was the Big Spring Recital in May, where every student had written, notated, and then performed their own original piece, plus played in an ensemble.

I think back on one such recital. The church looked lovely that year—two grand pianos gleamed on the stage; the black-ink notes of each original composition danced on the manuscript paper displayed on walls around the room, and the sanctuary overflowed with baskets of red geraniums.

There were more guests than I had expected; the students played their pieces well; the ensembles were charming; a joyful spirit filled the room.

At the end of the program, I stood on my head. The students and parents whooped and hollered.

(I had often stood on my head for the *students* at the last class of the year. Once a little student turned her head upside-down, looked at me, and remarked, "I have never known such a little old lady to be so spry." I was forty-seven at the time.)

I had not planned to make any closing remarks, but, as I prepared that morning, the following poem popped into my mind:

> *It is to this time that I have come*
> *to an afternoon such as this*
> *full of music, children,*
> *laughter, learning, joy*
>
> *It is to this time that I have come*
> *to claim my small space on the planet*
> *to share what I can do*
> *to stretch my talent*
> *to take a risk*
>
> *It is to this time that I have come*
> *but I could not be here without each of you*
> *sharing, loving, soothing*
> *Thank you so much!*

As we ate our cookies and drank our punch, the children and their parents beamed. Again, and again, the students came up and hugged me to say goodbye for the summer. As we embraced, I realized once more how much joy I find in teaching.

And, as I look back now, I know that without Dr. Pace's continued acumen, encouragement, and enlightenment, I could never have taught for those forty, mostly delightful years.

No Way

"*I can't believe my eyes—or ears!" I thought as I sat in a classroom the first afternoon of a three-day workshop at the University of Denver. "Surely these five-year-olds aren't playing a piece, then transposing it into Dorian mode, then improvising. No way!"* Arlyce Black was stupefied. In all her years of teaching she had seen nothing like this. She goes on:

Carolyn Heitzman, a fellow teacher from Foothills Music Teachers Association and Pacesetters, had invited me to go with her to meet Dr. Robert Pace and there he was, working with Dr. David Montano's five-year-old students in a most impressive and remarkable way.

After that workshop I attended every Master Class and Festival held in the Denver Area—Dr. Pace was an inspiration to all students and teachers.

He always carried a book. I felt it was a subtle way to encourage us to read and learn. I always bought whichever book right away. One that impressed me greatly was Mihaly Csikszentmihalyi's Flow: The Psychology of Optimal Experience. *It suggests that the secret to happiness is not found through money or success, but by immersing ourselves in something we love, by ordering the information that enters our consciousness, by sensing art-play-work as one.*

I loved Dr. Pace's explanation of Spiral Learning and his suggestion of a twenty-minute warm-up practice each day, whether you had access to a piano or not:

- *Double full diminished 7ths SLOW MOTION*
- *5-finger Hanon exercise*
- *Two Minute Major and Minor Scales*
- *Arpeggios*
- *Trill with weight & rhythms*
- *6ths and 3rds VERY SLOWLY*
- *Chromatic Scale*
- *Faster diminished 7ths*
- *Staccato Octaves*
- *Any other 5-Finger Hanon*

The idea of having each student participate in a group lesson was a life changer for most students. They could share their music and knowledge in a natural, weekly setting.

The Pacesetters group in Colorado was greatly strengthened by the rotation of Festivals: Improvisation, Composition, and Ensemble. We were also strengthened by participating in group learning twice a month ourselves. We focused on Classical, Jazz, improvisation, along with the basics of ear training, rhythms, etc. All teachers were willing to share their own experiences and knowledge without hesitation.

I noticed that the Festivals had better attendance when we used outside conductors and guest artists for the Festivals rather than our local Pace Teachers. The guests created more excitement for both the students and the teachers. While I still use materials from local teachers, I will always keep close at hand the notes from Dr. Pace, Marjorie Weist, and others.

I believe it was Dr. Pace who said, "You need to present the same idea thirteen times for the students to remember." Might it be the same for teachers?

– **Arlyce Black**

What's Not to Love?

The Composition Festivals were my favorite.

They were also a terrific amount of work for the teacher and the kids.

Although we teachers worked with our students on creativity and improvisation all the time, making an original composition, notating it, copying it in ink, and performing it at the Festival was a *big deal*.

As we studied our *Music for Piano* pieces, we learned to improvise on them, making little changes in the melody, making new melodies over the bass lines, changing the rhythm. The *Creative Music* books of the series had many additional exercises.

Even with all that, some students were prone to whine, "I can't write a piece. It won't be any good. The others will be better than mine. You can't make me do it." The latter was true, of course. So, cajoling and suggestions became the order of the weeks leading up to the festival.

Sometimes the copies were a bit smudged, but it was ink. We hired outside adjudicators, who studied the pieces beforehand, listened to the performances, and made kind, constructive comments.

The day of the Composition Festival was glorious—broad smiles, happy parents, tired teachers.

Many Pacesetter students won awards at various composition contests. Sometimes our teachers won all the awards. Not to brag or anything.

Quotes and Tips from Dr. Pace

- You can keep any child's attention for one minute; it just takes thirty of those one minutes. A student can concentrate on their practice for one minute. Just string together thirty of them.

- Teach variety in many ways—touch, style, musical problems, improvisation.

- With the dyad, both students are obligated to come prepared for every lesson; it's a matter of friendly competition.

- We need to distinguish between: growth and accumulation, going in circles and moving ahead, new material and old in disguise. New material expands previous concepts.

- Be patiently impatient with students.

- See with your ears, hear with your eyes.

- Ask your student: What are you going to do at home the rest of the week? Ask yourself: Am I teaching in a way that they will be able to continue at home?

- Forward motion comes from getting more satisfaction, deeper response; it doesn't have to come from harder and harder pieces.

- For the students with less technical prowess, rather than pushing beyond Books III or IV, broaden their repertoire, concentrate more on playing very musically.

- Teach students how to concentrate, not daydream and wiggle fingers.

- A scale is only how fast you can play two notes, then two more.

- Habit formation is the worst way to learn.

- 95% of rote learning never leaves the studio.

- We are in education to show students principles and problem-solving.

Dr. Pace teaching class

Please, Please, No

The phone rang just as I finished morning lessons. It was the mother of one of my students.

"Mrs. Hjelmstad. Mrs. Hjelmstad, I just want you to know that the Jabs have been in a terrible car accident."

The three Jabs children were all students of mine. Beautiful, blond, brown-eyed Jennie, who was going on sixteen, had recently decided to concentrate on her cello. Peter, tall, lanky, and Mensa-smart, was almost fourteen. Sweet little Ami had just turned eight.

"What? What?! Tell me, tell me quickly."

"Ami is here with us. She had a sleepover with our daughter. But the others…"

"Tell me."

"Mr. Jabs and Jennie are dead. Mrs. Jabs and Peter have severe head injuries. It's not sure they will live."

I was too stunned to talk.

Les and I rushed to their house to find Ami. Someone had just told her about her family. She ran into my arms, "Oh, thank you, thank you!" I held her close for a long, long time.

Les and I went to Denver General Hospital to see Barb and Peter. Sadness engulfed us. Later Peter was transferred to Craig Rehabilitation Hospital. He still couldn't walk or talk. He was like a long, limp strand of spaghetti.

One day I cautiously asked Peter if he could play for me. He just stared. I continued to talk softly, "Do you remember *The Entertainer*?" He nodded slightly. I took a deep breath.

"Do you think you could play it for me right now?" His attendant moved his wheelchair to the piano in the corner of the room.

Peter's hands moved to the keyboard. After a brief hesitation, the opening octaves of his favorite Scott Joplin rag rang out loud and clear. He played the entire piece without a glitch. The nurses and physical therapists clapped. I cried. At that point, music was the only thing that had not disappeared.

Both Mrs. Jabs and Peter eventually became physically functional, but their brain injuries limited their lives in many ways. Barbara was able to continue to enjoy singing in choirs, however, and her cheerful disposition was an inspiration to many of us. She sent cards for every and any occasion, beautifully decorated with a variety of stickers.

Peter's piano became a lifeline to some sense of normality, but, as a 6' 4", 350-pound adult with the to-be-expected anger and mental health issues, he struggled at times.

Little Ami resumed her lessons. Her group and I supported her in any way we could.

Dear Jennie was the only one of my students who died (although several had cancer diagnoses). At one of her memorial services, Barbara asked me to play *La Fille aux Cheveux de Lin*.

Although our contact in Ami's adult years had been a bit sporadic, Les and I did attend her wedding at the Stanley Hotel in Estes Park, Colorado. And later, Barbara sent me multiple pictures of the light of her life, her grandson, Mason. I was not surprised that Ami called me again when Mrs. Jabs died in late 2019.

In our long telephone conversation, we talked about the horror of the accident and how it changed their lives. She told me that Peter, now almost 50, is doing much better. He spends time with Ami, her husband, and their amazing son. And she said she wanted me to tell their story.

Peter still plays the piano—a medley of various pieces he studied, never quite the entirety of each piece, but skillfully stringing them together.

The details of the accident and the days following remain hazy to Ami—she was such a young child—but she said that one thing stands out in her mind from that ghastly day. She still has a clear picture of Les and me walking into the house where she sat, with people whom she did not know well, disoriented, dazed.

And she distinctly remembers thinking, "Thank God. It's Mrs. Hjelmstad. Someone I know. Someone who loves me."

As we talked, Ami reminded me that, in the days following the accident, her cat died; her dog was torn to pieces by a neighbor's dog. She lost everything.

And she said that, during the following days, weeks, months, years, music anchored her. Music and I were the only things that stayed the same in her life. Her words humbled me deeply. I had no idea.

Again, I cried.

Like Mother, Like Daughter

We each have come to teaching the Robert Pace Method in our own way. Kathy Van Arsdale, chairman of the Legacy Group, tells her story:

For several years, I had observed my mother, Ruth O'Neal, become more and more enthralled with a new philosophy of piano education offered by Dr. Robert Pace, of Columbia University. She had switched her entire studio to a partner and group system, met Dr. Pace several times in Aspen, and made the decision to study with him during the summer at Columbia University in New York, with other budding Pace teachers.

Since my undergraduate degree from the University of Colorado Boulder was in General Music Education with a K-12 teaching certification, I began my professional career teaching General Music in the classroom in Howard County, Maryland and Jefferson County, Colorado. I was chosen to conduct the All-County Elementary Choir and offered a contract to teach rural school classrooms having no music teacher, on TV.

When I became Orff-certified at three levels in Colorado, I designed a music classroom, and ordered instruments, books, and equipment for Little Elementary in Jefferson County.

After leaving classroom teaching behind, I was at home with a newborn, ready to begin my MA in Music Education at the University of Denver, when opportunity called: Ruth's very successful home studio had become larger than she and her Pace-certified assistant, Winnie Boyle, could handle.

Ruth asked me to teach one day a week—a Level I class plus two partner lessons. I began a Level I Pedagogy Course immediately. Although I felt unsure of my ability in my third musical instrument (my skills in voice and violin were stronger), I gave it a try. I soon found that my previous skills in lesson planning, classroom management, and music theory were an advantage to teaching the Pace method.

However, the real revelation was the Pace Philosophy.

The Level I course was most enlightening. My peers and I were amazed to learn that Dr. Pace had revolutionized the teaching style we encountered in college. We were fascinated to discover that he had, over many years, designed, employed, evaluated, refined, and revised learning materials and teaching concepts, as he used the Community Music Center at Columbia University as his lab. Learning that his goals and philosophy aligned with and affirmed my own thinking about music education astonished me.

Dr. Pace, realizing at Julliard that only about one hundred people earn a living performing classical piano concerts professionally, gave thought to his true calling—piano music education. This, too, paralleled my personal history: I rejected an undergraduate major in vocal performance, although pressured by many to attempt to sing professionally. I had been clear since middle school that music education was my calling.

Over the years, I attended many sessions designed to inform, inspire, and elevate the profession of piano instruction. Dr. Pace continued to expand on his remarkable innovative thinking regarding conceptual teaching:

- *spiral learning*
- *peer teaching and learning*
- *early introduction of higher-level thinking skills through improvisation and theory*
- *the use of ensemble*
- *implementation of multi-key, modal*
- *the twelve-tone scale and other contemporary composition technics.*

Dr. Pace had sequenced the learning and literature for us, so that we need have no fear of such a sophisticated and comprehensive methodology. Every notion was backed by research. With many like-minded teachers surrounding me, I was immersed in my implementation of the Pace philosophy and the vibrant local Pace group.

At the beginning of any session with teachers, consultants, conventioneers, or casual spectators, Dr. Pace articulated the way this philosophy is vital to impact the world for good.

He felt that students yearn to have the "peak experiences" described by Abraham Maslow (one of many psychologists, learning theorists, and educators often cited by Dr. Pace) and that the artistic beauty inherent in music can engender such experiences.

Students crave the acceptance and affirmation supplied by a music learning group. Students long to express themselves in original thinking, so prized by businesses and governments of the future. Their brains need the stimulation provided in musical performance.

Students seek the centering and peace provided by performing and listening to music. The joy of music will guide their thinking forever.

Over the years, I met Robert Pace dozens of times in formal and informal settings. One of my favorite memories is of my birthday party at The Fort restaurant overlooking Denver, featuring indigenous food. While they sang "Happy Birthday," Dr. Pace and my parents donned celebratory headgear. Dr. Pace's wore a large coyote head and skin. He snapped a photo to preserve the memory; it was passed around at several consultants' conferences to peals of laughter!

I presented Dr. Pace's philosophy of education to dozens of pedagogy classes, local professional associations, state conventions, local and state boards of directors, university pedagogy classes, national conventions, and international non-profit boards. I have written about Dr. Pace's ideas in local, state, and national publications, seeking to spread the word.

Like several other Pace consultants, including Dr. Cynthia Pace and Nan Beth Walton, I learned from a parent that Robert Pace's philosophy is an instrumental way to impact young lives.

– **Kathy Van Arsdale**

He Made Us Smile

Justin was part of my youngest Book One Group. He always tore down the basement stairs at breakneck speed, plopped his books on the piano rack, ready for business, and started dinking around on the keys.

We all loved Justin. He happily participated in everything. He ran to the blackboard to write key signatures. He lined up first to do flash cards. He raised his hand even as I asked a question.

After his lesson, he grabbed his books and ran for the door, shouting, "I'm outta hewo. I'm histowy."

Justin grew to be six foot four and majored in music. He now plays in a jazz band.

History of the 90s

The Soviet Union collapsed; the US conducted Operation Desert Storm in Iraq; William J. Clinton was elected twice and impeached once; Timothy McVeigh bombed and brought down the Alfred R. Murrah Building in Oklahoma City; twelve students and one teacher were shot and killed at Columbine High School in Littleton, Colorado, on April 20, 1999.

As teachers, we lived in that world. But in the world of Pace, we could escape to our studios and the students we loved. *Kinder-Keyboard* was published in 1991 and *Music for Moppets* came shortly after. Those books presented ways to engage rhythm and music in younger children, sooner.

Dr. Pace decided he could no longer travel to direct Ensemble Festivals.

In 1995-96, Consultant Kathleen Davis suggested restructuring the Study Groups so that they could be held at the General Meeting time. We hoped that these "Super Study Groups" would better meet the needs of our members and would be better attended.

Second Generation

New teachers came to join those of us who had been around since the beginnings of Pace in Colorado.

Cindy Allor was one of those. She jumped in with both feet and became a significant asset to our community. She personified the "second generation." We were grateful and lucky to have them. She responded to the call for stories with this:

Although I consider myself a "second-generation" Pacesetter teacher in the sense that I came to the plate late in my teaching career (mid-90s), I will be always grateful that I was able to benefit from Dr. Pace's pedagogy classes, his method books, and his inspiration.

Being a part of the community of Pace teachers in Colorado gave me hands-on insights as to the groundwork of teaching. I found much encouragement and guidance for my studio within the group and still hold these amazing teachers in high regard.

This was not a group to stumble by in the studio. This was a group of focused, concept-driven teachers who understood the power of and importance of well-rounded musicians. This was a method of not just teaching students, but learning alongside students, as well as learning how to teach. To that end, I am still in awe.

I was very excited to finally meet Dr. Pace in the late 90s, to observe his teaching, his compassion, his intuitiveness in helping students think critically, teach themselves, and learn from their fellow students as well as their teachers.

We have seen multiple examples of his influence in music method books written by others, in a rising awareness of composition as groundwork to learning music, and in his unique, focused approach to learning styles via the understanding of musical concepts as the foundation upon which to build.

To Dr. Pace, and to all those Pace teachers who brought his approach to fruition, I say thank you for your contribution to a more musical community, society, nation, and world.

*– **Cindy Allor***

A Trip to Rockley's Music Store

Les and I had spent Labor Day weekend at a cabin in the Colorado Rockies. On our way home, we took Colfax Avenue into Denver. Why? Because Rockley's Music Center was on West Colfax. I had finished scheduling and verifying all the lessons for the coming year. Rockley's was my next step. And I had my list.

First, I picked up a complete set of Dr. Pace's books: *Music for Piano, Creative Music, Finger Builders,* and *Theory Papers* for each of my students, whatever their level (One through Six). Then I looked for supplemental sheet music and collections to complement the basic books. I aimed to buy all the stuff I would need for the entire year. Nina Rockley didn't see me often, but that day she saw me for a long, long time.

I wrote a huge check and handed it to Nina. She who had ordered enough Pace material for the teachers in Colorado and beyond. She who had thoughtfully ordered additional material that she felt would be useful to us. She who had patiently helped each teacher as they came in.

Les carried the heavy boxes to the car. I could feel the "I'm so excited to begin teaching" feeling begin to rise. When we got home, I sorted the books and put them in order on the shelves in my studio, awaiting the sixty students who would begin, starting the following Monday.

The first week of classes, we "opened" the books, pressing down several pages at a time so that the books would lie flat on the piano racks. As the notes of new material popped on the pages in front of them, the students could scarcely contain their excitement.

There is no delight compared to that of new books. The sweet aroma of paper. The shiny covers, unmarred. The pages, crisp and unblemished.

We were all a bit giddy.

Dr. Pace on Creativity

*Creativity: taking the usual and
doing it in an unusual way*

*The more structured you are,
the more creative you can be*

*Our ultimate goal is to build a better world,
one student at a time*

*We are not teaching music.
We are teaching CHILDREN music*

Bad Dream, Good Ensembles

One night during the summer of 2019, after I had spent the day working on this book, I dreamt that I was at one of the Pace Ensemble Festivals.

The end of the program had come, and it was time for the teachers to perform. There were ten pianos and twenty teachers ready to play *Maria* from *West Side* Story. The teachers' performance was much anticipated by the students and parents.

Carolyn Heitzman was to play primo and I had been assigned to secondo. She put the music on the piano. I looked at the score. I had never seen it before. There was no way I could play it. I knew I couldn't even fake it.

I was red with embarrassment; my students and parents were watching. I stood up from the piano and hid behind the curtains of the stage.

Fortunately, I woke up and quit shaking.

In real life, the Ensemble Festivals were a lot of fun, even though I did find it challenging to play with such a large group. I wasn't accustomed to playing in ensembles.

However, the students were used to playing with others and following a conductor in their weekly Large Groups, so they looked forward with great anticipation to the Ensemble Festivals, especially in the years when Dr. Pace was guest conductor.

The parents glowed with pride to see their children perform. Some even brought bouquets of flowers for their students.

Several times we got local news coverage, probably because it was such a major effort and accomplishment to deliver such a concert.

Many of our teachers have said that they enjoyed the Ensemble Festivals the most.

However, when I asked Denise Lanning which event/events *she* relished the most, she wrote that *"my most inspiring moments came from the Master Classes that Dr. Pace held for teachers when he came to Denver for Ensemble and Creative Festivals."*

How and Why We Stayed Together

It was a unique experience to be part of the Colorado Pacesetters. We were all dedicated to teaching the same materials (with our own supplemental ideas and materials), in much the same manner. We were committed to offering partner lessons and Large Group classes every week. We were dedicated to having frequent group recitals to show what our students were learning, to help them feel comfortable performing, and to encourage their creativity.

Almost any problem we encountered had been experienced by at least one other teacher in the group. We could be supportive in ways other teachers could not. We were collaborative, rather than competitive.

For many years we participated in Study Groups twice monthly. In those groups we taught one another the Pace material in much the same way as we taught our students. We formed lines with one teacher asking a musical question and the next person in line answering it. We learned to think on our feet.

The *Colorado Pacesetters Newsletter* kept us apprised of ideas, events, and some of the happenings in our musical and personal lives.

At some point, we began hosting Pace Festivals in a three-year rotation:

Creative and Fundamentals
Composition
Ensemble Workshops.

There is a chart for some of the Festivals in the Appendices.

We stayed together—the basic philosophies, the why's, the how's held us together. We had common goals and a common way to reach them.

Five Girls and a Baby

One August I answered my phone to hear Wendy's mother say, "Mrs. Hjelmstad, we need to come see you before the fall lessons start."

I was in the middle of scheduling for the year, but I said, "Yes, of course."

Several days later the two of them walked into the studio, looking very serious. After some small talk, Mrs. Newton said, "I know you've already scheduled Wendy's class and partner, but we don't know what to do about lessons this fall." There was a moment before she continued. "Wendy is pregnant."

Whoa. Wendy would be a senior. She was due in February. It would be a tough year.

"We don't know how you or the girls will feel about her being in class. "

I caught my breath.

"I would be fine, but I will check with the other four girls and their parents."

Each of the discussions heartened me. Everyone agreed that we'd love for Wendy to remain.

Mrs. Newton said that she didn't much care if any music happened, she just wanted her daughter to be with us.

The young man who had impregnated her offered and begged, "I'll sell my stereo to pay for the abortion. Just, please, please, please don't tell my parents."

Under no circumstances, tempted as she might be, would Wendy have an abortion, so she tried to come to grips with giving up her baby for adoption. The decision-making was grueling. Wendy and I talked and cried a lot. But as soon as she had decided, for absolute sure, her parents stepped up to adopt the child.

Throughout the pregnancy, birth, and beyond, the other girls were solicitous and supportive. One day at Large Group we had a nice shower for Wendy. The girls brought gifts. We had a cake, cups of punch, and mixed nuts.

When Wendy's beautiful little son was born, she held him, nursed him. In the end she couldn't give him up, even to her parents. With their help she finished high school, then college. She subsequently married an incredible man. Together they gave two brothers to her son. I still get Christmas cards with pictures. Her baby is a wonderful human.

When I asked for permission to share her story, Wendy emailed me:

I love the story. No changes or additions. I'm so grateful for the support that I got to hold me upright!

I'm honored that you even thought to write this story. Thank you over and again for all your love and support during that time. The shower that you all threw me was such a surprise. I think back on it often.

At a time when I did not feel worthy, the love and kindness showed by you and my fellow students overwhelmed me. Thank you, thank you, thank you!

Love and hugs,
Wendy

History of the 2000s

The 2000s brought events in our country that included: George W. Bush was president for two terms; the Twin Towers came down; the space shuttle Columbia blew up; Hurricane Katrina devastated New Orleans; the school shootings continued apace; Barack Obama became president.

We Pacesetters mainly kept on keeping on. Some interesting things showed up in the minutes:

In 2001 Hazel Roberts Ramsbotham attended the International Music Festival in Australia. Kathy Van Arsdale went to Italy for a concert tour with her high school mixed choir. Denise Lanning judged the regional organ contest in Fargo, North Dakota. Debbie Berwick and Cindy Allor successfully completed their first Summer Piano Camp. Darlene Harmon attended the Van Cliburn competition.

The Creative Festival in 2002 with Dr. Pace had 177 registered participants with only thirteen no-shows. Dr. Pace evaluated that event as follows:

Over the years, the Denver Pacesetter Program has been one of the best in the country. Student performances are consistently good—both technically and musically. Also, the teachers' performances during our Master Classes give evidence of good musicianship and a desire to continue professional growth.

The by-laws committee reported that "membership remains constant and strong. New Pacesetters are added annually."

Pacesetters dues were raised to $20.00.

The 2005 Fundamentals Festival was held at the Community College of Aurora.

In 2006 Hazel Ramsbotham was named Teacher of the Year in Colorado. The next year she was recognized at the National Certification Gala as the teacher with MTNA's longest-standing Professional Certification.

Dr. Pace was recognized at the 2007 MTNA Conference in Austin, Texas. Carolyn Shaak and Jim Lyke praised him for his innovative leadership and contributions.

Kathy Van Arsdale had the honor of presenting at the 2008 MTNA National Convention in Denver.

But, as the decade wore on, we Pacesetters began to feel ourselves dwindling from the heydays of the 1970s, 80s, and even the 90s.

Lexi and Dr. Pace

The day I was planning to send this manuscript to the editor, Bonnie Early emailed this story. I'm glad she beat the deadline:

> During the 80s and 90s, it was a thrill for my regular students to know that, sooner or later, they would have a chance to meet and work with the inimitable Dr. Pace.
>
> The last time I saw Dr. Pace was during the MTNA Convention in Colorado in the 2000s. He gave several workshops that exhibited his group teaching method, using local students.
>
> I entered little Lexi, who was only six years old, in the Level 1 Class demonstration. I knew that she barely understood what was going on, but, as I told her parents, it was unlikely that she would ever have another chance to work with Dr. Pace. It was almost certainly the last time any of the students would have that opportunity. Sadly, I was correct.
>
> The parent of another student had planned to videotape Lexi's session, but he got stuck in traffic and didn't arrive until the class was over. So, we improvised; I interviewed Dr. Pace as the parent taped for fifteen minutes. In the end, it was easier to tape an interview than a class session. Dr. Pace's answers to focused questions were probably more valuable, anyway.
>
> But Lexi got to see Dr. Pace, and work with him. And her parents were thrilled, as she also may well be in retrospect.
>
> – **Bonnie Early**

Some Reasons Why We Began to Fade

As the Colorado Pacesetters look back over the thousands of lessons we have collectively given, the exciting festivals, the fulfilling work we have done and are doing, we feel great sadness as we realize that our Pacesetters and the Pace Comprehensive Musicianship Method is fading in Colorado and across the nation.

Why has this happened?

We brainstormed at one of the Legacy meetings and came up with some possibilities:

- The Pace Method requires a lot of time and effort, particularly in setting it up in your studio for the first year. It demands figuring out a schedule that includes appropriate partner lessons, suitable groupings of the dyads in a large group setting, and proper lesson planning, preferably for the entire academic year. I needed plenty of Excedrin when I started that first August.

- Every week we teachers need to plan both the partner lessons and the Large Group lessons. We must choose repertoire that complements the concepts we are presenting.

- Writing a policy for our studios takes time, too, and billing for the term can be onerous. (We found that charging for each semester, just as private schools do, eliminated missed and tardy lessons.)

- Many teachers saw it as being too much work and taking too much time, even though they were convinced that the Pace Method was far superior to private lessons.

- Over the more than fifty years since the Colorado Pacesetters began, we noticed that additional activities encroached on the days that lessons could be scheduled. As busyness became a badge of honor ("Our life is just *crazy!*" parents moaned), more and more appointments were added—football, soccer, dance, art, you name it. It became harder and harder to make a reasonable schedule; practice time became acutely crunched.

- The culture gradually changed, too. Making music oneself became less important. Immediate music was instantaneously available. Piano sales slumped. The pool of potential students diminished.

- Other methods began including more theory and creativity, especially in approaches from those who had studied with Dr. Pace as graduate students.

- The Denver Area Music Teachers and other music groups also lost participants.

- In the 1970s and 80s, the consultants could always rustle up a group to teach. But that changed in the 90s and going forward.

- When Dr. Pace created his program, the options for learning and entertainment were fewer. It's a different world now.

- The level of competency required to organize and teach this method required bright individuals, and bright individuals have the competency to take on new ventures. Some of them did.

- Dr. Pace got older and older. The rest of us did not have his charisma. We tried, but he was a hard act to follow.

History of the 2010s

The Digital Age advanced worldwide with things like smartphones and Instagram; the thirty-year shuttle program ended at the Kennedy Space Center; mass shootings continued with the twenty-six deaths at Sandy Hook being especially egregious; same-sex marriage was legalized in all fifty United States; Donald Trump became president; Hurricane Maria ruined Puerto Rico; the #MeToo movement swept the country.

Perhaps in response to some of these shifts, the International Piano Teaching Foundation found itself less stringent in its suggested regulations for membership, certification, festivals, and peer-studio observance.

Even though Dr. Pace himself had championed strict adherence to the guidelines in order to elevate the profession in general, our Colorado Pacesetter board now suggested that we mirror IPTF's current thinking, in which local groups pretty much welcome anyone who wants to join, pay dues, and learn. While, ideally, we'd want members to adhere to the stricter rubrics, the world and times were changing around us.

Our Pacesetter president observed: *We currently have inactive members, members who pick and choose the Festivals in which to participate, what part of the Pace approach to employ. My guess is that 20% of our members meet the "Gold Standard," which is: every student to participate in partner and group lessons weekly, every student to attend every Festival, and every teacher certified as having completed a Comprehensive Musicianship Course for every level that they teach.*

We Lost Our Mentor

We were all deeply saddened when Dr. Pace died in October 2010. At our meeting that month, Kathleen Davis reflected on his passing. She shared that he was the one who had made her what she is today. Others also told how he had revolutionized piano teaching and changed their lives. This book pays homage to his genius.

His influence is well represented in those he taught: James and Jane Bastien, Randall and Nancy Faber, Walter and Carol Noona, Bernard and Carolyn Schaak, Robert Vandall—the great educators of our times.

In correspondence with Kathy Van Arsdale, Dr. Cynthia Pace related that her father had often affirmed our group as a model for others and applauded our persistence and tenacity. Cindy thanked us for our dedication. It meant a lot to him.

Yes, we deeply mourn Dr. Robert Pace. However, his legacy and our teaching has influenced thousands and thousands of teachers and students and in that we are comforted.

But Even as We Faded…

When I reviewed the 2000-2018 minutes of our meetings, it became obvious that the students of Pace teachers continued to win awards and contests; many of our students have remained involved in music in various ways.

Although I'm sure this is not a comprehensive list, I'll share the items that were in the notes. We don't need dates, do we?

One of Arlyce Black's students won the Junior High Division of CSMTA Composition contest, four performed in the Clementi Festival, two prior students are now working in music departments at the college level.

Kerry Cottingham reported that her nephew is moving to Denver and will be teaching piano. Her niece also will move to Denver to help with the PR at Kerry's Colorado Music Institute.

Bonnie Early's home-schooled piano students put together a music program using rhythm instruments and performed for thirty people. Two of her students won the composition competition at the National Creative Festival and one even won the MTNA competition.

Bonnie also told the story of two former students (one from the 90s and one from the early 2000s) who returned in 2019 with their children.

The parents were excited for those kids to have the opportunity to learn under the Pace method, just as *they* once had. They shared fond memories from their own lessons with

Bonnie. She added that Pace teachers have always worked and studied hard to master comprehensive teaching; it has made a difference in the lives of our students.

At one meeting, Ruth O'Neal shared that her student and grandson (Kathy Van Arsdale's son), Mark Van Arsdale, had given his high school senior voice recital. Mark went on to perform all over Europe and in the United States. Ruth also told us that one of her graduates had won a wonderful scholarship at DU.

Hazel Rambotham's fourteen-year-old piano student did a professionally recorded CD. Hazel had five students who performed in the Clementi Festival. Her former student Jason Gery took a DMA from Yale in musicology.

And as to further secondary reaches of piano students and their abilities to learn, I was happy to report that my grandson, Douglas Ball, had received a Fulbright scholarship to get his doctorate in linguistics from Stanford.

While getting his undergraduate degree at the University of Rochester, Doug had taken classes in composition at Eastman School of Music, right there on the other side of town. He still composes contemporary pieces for ensembles and orchestras, even as a linguistics professor.

Kathleen Davis tells the story of her student, Donya, who began lessons when she was four. Donya was precocious. Within a year she had become part of Kathleen's *middle* school piano group, and was accepted by them, and doing very well. The little girl was obsessed with dinosaurs, and, for several years, she came to lessons with a dinosaur tail pinned onto the back of her jeans.

Donya became a prolific composer for the keyboard and, the last Kathleen heard, she was at Harvard, working on electronic composition.

And then there is this little anecdote:

In the spring of 2019, another of my grandsons, Robert M. Hjelmstad, took his DMA from the University of Colorado. That fall he substituted for his mentor, David Korevaar, who was on sabbatical.

Although Robert's father, as a teenager, had gone through several years of the Pace program with me, I take no credit whatsoever for Robert. I never gave him a single lesson, although I practiced with him during our twice-a-year visits to Michigan.

And there was that time when I said, "You know what? You may have some talent. What if you practiced for thirty minutes? No drinks of water. No checking the weather. No playing with your dogs. Then, what if you upped that to forty-five minutes?"

I Teach, Therefore I Am

While perusing the many *Pacesetter Newsletters*, I came across this profound piece that Kathleen Davis had written after she retired from active teaching:

> This is a time in my life when I find it important to reflect on the big picture regarding many things. So, as I began to muse on this article, a twist on a familiar quote came to mind. "I TEACH, THEREFORE I AM." Think about it with me. How has teaching Comprehensive Musicianship shaped you and me —who we are and how we approach and affect the world in which we live?
>
> I find myself using the skills of Conceptual Thinking, Spiral Learning, Peer Learning, and facilitating as a teacher, even though I no longer see students daily. What a gift that is! And I am grateful that I have been able to give that gift to many teachers and hundreds of students over the years.
>
> We were teaching, not just piano, but musicianship, logic, patterns. It was the thinking person's method. We developed the whole person.
>
> **– Kathleen Davis**

Group Reunion

One afternoon, quite a while after I had retired from teaching and begun my writing and speaking career, I sat by my front bay window, drinking peach tea.

Glancing out to the yard, I was surprised to see half a dozen adults sitting in a circle under the large maple tree. Right there on the grass. As I looked more closely, I recognized some of their faces.

I dashed out to the lawn to greet my former students. "I'm so glad to see you, but what are you doing *here*?" I asked, as we melted into hugs.

"We wanted to get together and we all knew how to find your house."

Close the Gate Gently

It was a magical kingdom we fashioned,
the children and I,
through music and love and years of sharing

I reigned in a realm that was my own—
four walls and two small windows
messy chalkboards and long tables
rickety chairs and pretty posters
learning and laughter

I was the princess;
they were my friends
and together we could do anything

The Big Spring Recital was a coronation
a ritual that marked the renewal of our vows
The flowers and music validated the pledge
of mutual admiration and respect
(cont.)

Each child donned a robe of majesty
and wore a crown of courage

It was a magical kingdom—
emblem of my emergence
symbol of subsumation forsaken

And now I take off my tiara—
its stars shining as brightly
as the tears in my eyes—

and close the gate gently behind me

and close the gate gently behind me

(Excerpted from *This Path We Share*
©2010 Lois Tschetter Hjelmstad
Used by permission of Mulberry Hill Press)

Appendix 1

Consultants

Bonnie Cannalte – 1963, resigned October 1973, died 1980

Delta Bement – 1974

Ruth O' Neal – 1974

Janet Arnold came from Houston in 1976

Kathleen Davis – 1975

Lucille Koenig, Colorado Springs – 1982

Vicky Hammond, Colorado Springs – 1983

Kathy Van Arsdale – 1984

Appendix 2

HOW TO ORGANIZE YOUR STUDIO TO TEACH THE ROBERT PACE APPROACH

OR

WHAT TO DO AFTER THE DOCTOR COMES!!!

Lois Hjelmstad
Englewood, CO
1972

I. <u>One-Time Only Actions</u>

    a. <u>Burn all your bridges</u>. A compromise of several approaches won't work! If you have doubts, at least try this 100% with one group for a year and then compare results with any other approaches or series you might wish. But at least give this a chance to work first undiluted and uncompromised. Cross that bridge and decide that you will make this work!

    b. <u>Check your teaching environment.</u> Equip your studio with one or more well-action-regulated pianos, a blackboard, file cabinet, bulletin-board area and chairs. Prepare a policy statement and set up your billing system.

c. **Develop the habit of planning ahead**, So-o-o, pick up your pencil. This is the hardest step, whether it is the first time, every week, or every six weeks! But don't cut corners on this.

d. **Make your own master plan for each set of books.** Dr. Pace's approach encourages every teacher to use her own creative thinking. The books are your basic structure from which you constantly find new and more exciting teaching ideas.

Space out MP & CM** pages; find basic concepts presented on each page. Then correlate material in all areas, including seminar notes. Use large sheets of paper with headings like this:

Bk II	MP	SD	Ear Training	Creativity	Fundamentals	Chords	Technic
1st Week	p. 2	p.2	Intervals	Q & A	Key Signatures	I and V	Hanon
2nd Week	p.3	p.3	triads	Scales — up, down	Note names	IV	
3rd Week Etc.							

e. **Set up a small, three-ring notebook** with dividers for each large group you have. (The size that uses 9 ½ x 6 paper is compact and convenient.) In this notebook you will keep the yearly plans for each group, plus the current Six-Weeks Recital Plan, the current Partner Sheet, and the Large Group Lesson Plans.

II. Every Summer

a. <u>Make six sets of Teacher's Assignment Records</u> (printed by Lee Roberts Music Publications) for each group, one for each six-week period. Fill in spaced out MP & SD pages under the heading called sight reading and transposition. These become the year's plan for each group.

b. <u>Make a tentative master recital plan for the year.</u> From the information in IIa, you will be able to see what material and concepts fall into each six-week period. While the recitals will be based on those materials and concepts, you will have an endless variety of materials and ideas to present. Also, plan other projects, such as serial compositions, jazz improvisations, baroque composers, etc., and choose six-weeks periods to fit them in. An easy way to organize this material is as follows:

Recital Weeks	October 6	November 19	Etc., Dates for All Four - Six Recitals
Group Spacing (to see at a glance what concepts are in each six-weeks period)	Group 1 - MP IV 2-6* Grp 2 - MP III 2-7 Grp 3 - MP II 2-9 Grp 4- MP I 1-12	Group 1- MP IV 7-12 2 - MP III 8-14 3 - MP II 10-16 4 - MP I 13-18	*MP IV 2-6 means Music for Piano, Level 4, pages 2-6, etc.
Fundamentals	Grp 1 - Cadences Grp 2 - Aug. Triads 3 - Major Keys 4 - Note Names	1 - II Chord 2 - Octave Scale 3 - IV Chord 4 - ♯ & ♭	

Improvisations	1 - MP IV ideas 2 - MP III 2 3 - MP II 2-var. 4 - MP 2-7-var.	1 - MP IV 7 2 - MPIII 9 Triads 3 - MP II 10, 11 4 - Variations	
Ensemble	1 - MP IV 7 2 - MP III 3 3 - MP II 8 4 - MP I 6	1 - MP IV 10-12 2 - MP III 10-12 3 - MP II 13, 15 4 - MP I 15	
Solos (only list type here)	Group 1 - Classic 2 - Folk 3 - Echo Songs 4 - MP pieces	Group 1 - tie in 3rds & Scales 2 - Contemporary sounds (Recital Series) 3 - Contemporary (Recital Series) 4 - MP& Blue Recital Series	
P.R. (same for each group that week)	Talk about Goals: Literacy Creativity (Spiral learning vs. Showy pieces)	How to practice: Suggestions Encouragement	

*In this instance the Large Groups are numbered from the oldest groups (Group 1 is the oldest students) to the youngest. The first and second recital weeks are filled in as examples.

**MP stands for Music for Piano, CM for Creative Music, FB for Finger Builders, and TP for Theory Papers.

c. <u>Make six sets of six-weeks Recital Plans</u> for each group. A chart like this, made across the long way of the notebook paper, works well:

Group singing - fill in
Fundamentals -
Improvisation -
Ensembles -
Solos – (here you list each child's individual solo or solos)
Susie -   Bill -
Johnny -   Karen -

    d. <u>Make six sets of Partner Sheets</u> for each group. Simply divide sheets of notebook paper into as many squares as there are sets of partners in this group. These sheets are placed in the notebook directly opposite from current Six-Weeks Teachers' Assignment Guide and used to list items that would be separate from the basic material everyone receives, i.e., solos, special instructions, problems specific to the partners.

    e. <u>Make a calendar</u> for the year, listing recital dates and vacations.

III. <u>Every Six Weeks</u>

    a. <u>Fill in Six-Weeks Recital Plan</u>, using main ideas from Master Recital Plan, completing details.

    b. <u>Assign Solos</u>. Fill in on Partner Sheets.

    c. <u>Complete the details on Teachers' Assignment Guides</u> and make minor adjustments.

    d. <u>Plan creative projects</u> in sequence for the six weeks.
    e. <u>Remove previous Six-Weeks Recital Plan</u>, Partner Sheet, Large Group Plans from notebook, staple together, and file.

IV. <u>Every Week</u>

    a. Pick up the pencil the first thing Monday morning and do the planning for the entire week. It works wonders for your attitude!
    b. <u>Make Large Group Lesson Plan</u> from Teacher Assignment Guide, following Basic Format, Teachers Manual, page 5.
    c. <u>Make basic student assignment</u>, one for each group, from Teachers' Assignment Guide. (Use standard Pace Assignment Card.) Staple to the back of the Group Lesson Plan for your records.
    d. <u>Type copies of the above for each student</u> in each group. If good quality carbon paper is used, three copies may be made at once. (If only I had had my computer.)
    e. <u>Stack the assignment sheets chronologically</u>, so the first partners on Monday are at the top of the pile and the last partners on Friday on the bottom.

Appendix 2 | 129

V. Every Day

    a. <u>Straighten studio</u>; stack flash cards.

    b. <u>Go over the Large Group Lesson Plan</u> for that day in the morning and let it simmer in your sub-conscious during the day.

VI. Every Minute

    a. <u>Be confident</u> in the comprehensiveness of this approach.

    b. <u>Feel exhilarated</u> that you know exactly what you are doing!

    c. <u>Love</u> the kids and enjoy your time with them! You are bound to get good results.

NOTEBOOK

Teachers' Assignment Guides						
Date	Ex.	Scales	E.T*.	CM	MP	Fund	Chords
9/14							
9/21							
9/28							
10/5							
10/12							
10/19							

John / Sue	Fred / Pete	Alice / Joan
Bill / Nick	Jan / Betty	Ensembles

*Ear Training

These pages are open to one another in the notebook. The six-weeks Recital Plan is beneath the Partner Sheet for easy references. The Group Lesson Plans are added, in order, for six weeks. Then everything is removed, and we start over.

Appendix 3

Partial List of Dr. Pace's Visits to the West

1963 – Seminar at University of Denver

1968 – Fantastic two weeks in Aspen, Colorado (Lois Hjelmstad, Irene Jurgensen, Carol Watson)

1969 – One week in Aspen (Lois Hjelmstad, Ruth O'Neil, Pat Morrow)

???? – Another one or two weeks at Snowmass, Colorado (Delta Bement, Lois Hjelmstad)

1970 – Two weeks in Snowmass (Lois Hjelmstad, Pat Murrow, Rosa Silver)

1971 – One day in Boulder with pre-school materials

1972 – June 23 at the University of Denver

1974 – Lincoln, Nebraska (Jan Austin, Peggy Deel, Lois Hjelmstad, Ruth O'Neal)

June 9, 1977 – Colorado Women's College, Denver, Colorado

July 31, 1977 – one week in Santa Fe, New Mexico (Lois Hjelmstad, Susan Rudosky, others?)

June 1981 – Colorado Women's College, Denver, Colorado

Appendix 4

Sampling of PACE Festivals

Year	Facilitator	Location	Students	Teachers
1976	Dr. Pace	Ensemble Festival Thomas Jefferson HS		
1978		8th Annual Creative Musicianship Festival		
1981		Creative Festival Colorado Women's College		
1984	Mary Verne? Marvin Drucker, Gloria Burnett?	Creative Workshop		
1985		Composition Workshop		
1986	Dr. Pace	Ensemble Festival, Geo. Washington HS, Denver		
1989	Dr. Pace	Ensemble Festival Loretto Heights	350	26
1992	Dr. Pace	Ensemble Festival Montbello	294	21
1995	Marjorie Wiest	Ensemble Festival Montbello High	234	11
1998	Dr. Pace	Montbello High Ensemble Festival	205	12
2001	Marjorie Wiest	Ensemble Festival Montbello High	178	15
2002	Dr. Pace	Improvisation Festival		

Sampling of PACE Festivals

Year	Conductor(s)	Festival		
2003	Dr. Thomas Brosh	Creative Festival Montbello High	179	13
2004	Kathy Van Arsdale	Ensemble Festival Montbello High	179	13
2005		Fundamentals Fiesta		
2006	Kathy/Mike Raynes with Percussion	Composition Festival Montbello High	114	12
2007	Kathy/Mike Raynes Percussion Ensemble	Ensemble Festival Montbello High	114	12
2008	Jeremy Dittus	Improvisation Festival, Community College of Aurora		
2009	Grace Christus	Composition Festival Montbello High	97	11
2010	7 Teacher Conductors	Montbello High	97	11
2011	Hazel Ramsbotham	Creative Festival	93	
2012	Teacher Conductors	St. Andrews Methodist Church in Highlands	84	
2013	Kathy Van Arsdale, Kerry Cottingham, Kathleen Davis, Bonnie Early, Darlene Harmon, Hazel Ramsbotham	St. Andrews Methodist Church in Highlands	99	

Sampling of PACE Festivals

2014	Hazel Ramsbotham, Arlyce Black	Creative Festival	89	
2015	URI Ayn Rovner	Composition Festival	64	12
		UMC St. Andrews		
2016	5 Teacher Conductors	Washington Park United Church of Christ	41	12

Acknowledgments

I offer my deepest gratitude to:

- my editor, Barbara Munson, for her precise editing and thoughtful suggestions
- my designer, Nick Zelinger, who has made the book beautiful and easily digestible
- the Pace Legacy Group: Cindy Allor, Delta Bement, Arlyce Black, Kerry Cottingham, Kathleen Davis, Bonnie Early, Darlene Harmon, Denise Lanning, Ruth O'Neal, Susan Rudosky, Cheryl Scherer, and Kathy Van Arsdale, who supported, inspired, and cheered me on
- Ami Robertson and Wendy Holden, who allowed me to share their important, intimate stories
- my Writers' Group for their unwavering faith in me
- my children and grandchildren for their encouragement and unconditional backing
- my beloved husband, now 98 years old, who has forever been the Rock of Gibraltar around whom I have danced

About the Author

Lois Hjelmstad has authored four previous award-winning books, as well as numerous articles. She has spoken—in all fifty United States, Canada, and England—more than 600 times.

Lois lives with her husband, Les, in Englewood, Colorado, where she taught music for forty years. Les and Lois celebrated their 71st wedding anniversary on September 12, 2019. They have four children, eleven grandchildren, eight great-grandchildren, and one great-great-grandchild, plus in-laws. All are much-loved.

Her mission is to bring clarity, validation, courage, and solace to others.

Visit Lois at *http://www.loishjelmstad.com*